TOKYO

MEW MEW

A LA MODE

Tokyo Mew Mew a la Mode Vol. 1
Art by Mia Ikumi
Original Concept by Kodansha

Translation - Yoohae Yang
English Adaptation - Stuart Hazleton
Associate Editor - Peter Ahlstrom
Retouch and Lettering - Irene Woori Choi
Production Artist - Jason Milligan
Cover Design - Steven Chao

Editor - Carol Fox
Digital Imaging Manager - Chris Buford
Production Managers - Jennifer Miller and Mutsumi Miyazaki
Managing Editor - Lindsey Johnston
VP of Production - Ron Klamert
Publisher and E.I.C. - Mike Kiley
President and C.O.O. - John Parker
C.E.O. - Stuart Levy

A **TOKYOPOP**® Manga

TOKYOPOP Inc.
5900 Wilshire Blvd. Suite 2000
Los Angeles, CA 90036

E-mail: info@TOKYOPOP.com
Come visit us online at www.TOKYOPOP.com

ISBN: 1-59816-485-6

First TOKYOPOP printing: December 2005
10 9 8 7 6 5 4 3 2 1
Printed in the USA

TOKYO MEW MEW A LA MODE

™

ART BY MIA IKUMI
ORIGINAL CONCEPT BY KODANSHA

VOLUME 1

TOKYOPOP®

HAMBURG // LONDON // LOS ANGELES // TOKYO

9

YOU MEAN THAT DATA?

YES.

KEIICHIROU... I'M A LITTLE CONCERNED ABOUT THE NEW MOVEMENT.

THANKS.

HERE'S YOUR HOT CHOCOLATE, RYOU.

WOULD YOU LIKE ME TO START RESEARCHING A DNA MATCH?

IT COULD BE AN ERROR, BUT...

I'VE DISCOVERED SOME DISTRESSING DATA ABOUT MORE CHIMERA ANIMA IN SOME AREAS OF THE CAPITAL.

BUT FIRST...

Beep Beep

...LET'S TAKE CARE OF THE ALIEN IN FRONT OF US.

YES, RIGHT AWAY. LOOKS LIKE WE'LL HAVE TO HURRY UP...

...AND BEGIN A NEW MEW PROJECT.

LET'S KICK BUTT FOR THE FUTURE OF OUR PLANET!

YES!

HERE WE ARE!!

KICKIN'!

AH HA HA...

FOR SOME REASON, I'M JUST NOT AS EXCITED AS I USED TO GET.

1

In this space, I'd like to show you some illustrations from the 2004 Tokyo Mew Mew Calendar. It's called "Big Edo Mew Mew" (Laugh). Unfortunately, the calendar has already sold out. So for those who couldn't get it, enjoy the pics!

Princess Berry

Wah!

THE WEATHER IS JUST FABULOUS.

BERRY, WOULD YOU LIKE TO WALK HOME WITH US?

School's finally over for today!

Chauffeured?

SOMETIMES, ON A BEAUTIFUL DAY LIKE THIS, I LIKE TO WALK HOME INSTEAD OF BEING CHAUFFEURED!

TH-THAT SOUNDS WONDERFUL, KAORUKO.

The only "Niis" I've ever seen is a hot spring named that here in Japan!

Umm...sure...yeah. Totally!

Do you often go to Nice?

By the way, Berry, your grandfather is French, isn't he?

Umm yeah!

It's so warm for April. This reminds me of Nice in France.

I didn't check up on anything about this school except the uniform...

Meow!

I had no idea everyone here was so rich!

Oh no...

Pretending she's just as rich!

16

Yo!

BERRY!!

I came to pick you up. ♥

TASUKU!!

WHY ARE YOU HERE?!

WHY WOULD I MISS YOU?!

I THOUGHT YOU MUST BE MISSING ME BY NOW.

It took me forever to get here, even with a shortcut.

HOW DO YOU DO? NICE TO MEET YOU. TASUKU MEGURO, AT YOUR SERVICE.

Please call me Tasuku.

BERRY? IS THIS AN ACQUAINTANCE OF YOURS?

WELL... YES... BUT...

LADIES-- HOPE TO SEE YOU AGAIN SOON! ♡

N-NICE TO MEET YOU, TASUKU!

WELL, I'M GLAD YOU MADE SOME FRIENDS TO WALK HOME WITH.

I WAS JUST WORRIED THAT YOU WERE LONELY...

GUESS I'LL HEAD BACK NOW.

I JUST SAID I WASN'T!

WHAT A GENTLE-MAN...

OH... HE'S GONE.

WHAT DID YOU SAY?!

WELL, UNTIL TOMOR-ROW.

SEE YOU THEN!

...

AND SUCH GRACE AND MANNERS!

HE'S LIKE THE ANGEL MICHAEL...

How could he possibly be popular with these girls?!

Why?!

THOSE LOOKS, THAT STYLE!

HE'S LIKE A GREEK SCULPTURE COME TO LIFE, DON'T YOU THINK?

MY TRAIN RIDE TAKES AN HOUR, AND HE THINKS IT'S COOL TO ROLLERBLADE THAT FAR? IDIOT...

WHAT COULD THEY POSSIBLY MEAN BY "THOSE LOOKS, THAT STYLE"?

ぶん

ぶんっ

．．．．．．

THOUGH I GUESS IF I INCLUDE THE TIME IT TAKES ME TO WALK FROM THE TRAIN STATION, THE DIFFERENCE ISN'T REALLY THAT MUCH...

I'M GLAD YOU MADE SOME FRIENDS TO WALK HOME WITH.

But...

...I gotta admit that was kinda cool.

He came on rollerblades to see me and then just left like that...

21

YOU ALL
RIGHT?

Wha?
Huh?
Eeeeeh?!

WELL...
UM...

22

YOU'RE LATE!

SORRY.

MY DRAMA SHOOT WAS DELAYED.

OH! I'M WATCHING THAT! IT'S THE ONE AT 10 P.M. ON TUESDAYS, RIGHT?

SHALL WE START? MY TIME IS PRECIOUS.

OH QUIET, YOU.

YES.

IS THIS THE ONE YOU WERE TALKING ABOUT?

SIX MONTHS AGO, THE ALIENS RETREATED FROM EARTH, LEAVING THESE CREATURES BEHIND.

BUT THEY'RE BEING ELIMINATED...

...BY THE MEMBERS OF TOKYO MEW MEW.

ONCE THEY'RE GONE, WE CAN REBUILD THIS BORING GROWNUP WORLD INTO OUR OWN UTOPIA... SHANGRI-LA.

THEY CARELESSLY BLOCK THE PATH TO OUR GOALS.

THEY'LL HINDER OUR PROGRESS.

WELL THEN, ELIMINATE THEM.

INDEED.

ANYTHING AND EVERYTHING THAT STANDS IN OUR WAY SHALL BE WIPED OUT!

YES. WE SHALL RESHAPE THIS WORLD THROUGH OUR INTELLIGENCE, PHILANTHROPY, AND ELEGANCE!

YES, DUKE.

Ears? A tail? What the--?

What's going on?!

Me...a Mew Mew?

A Mew Mew...

What?

YOU...

...but isn't Tokyo Mew Mew the ones who were fighting those aliens?

....JUST BECAME A MEW MEW.

You've gotta be kidding me!

Ahhh! My head!

HEY, DID YOU HEAR WHAT I JUST SAID?

She's not paying attention at all...

Wait a minute-- this place is called Café Mew Mew!

BUT WHAT'S DONE IS DONE, SO WE'LL JUST HAVE TO DEAL...

Ah!

I saw Tokyo Mew Mew on TV once.

...WHAT JUST HAPPENED ISN'T SOME- THING WE PLANNED FOR.

But I'm...just a normal girl!!

LOOK, I UNDERSTAND YOU MUST BE IN SHOCK....

...I'm feeling super dizzy...

Suddenly...

SHE FAINTED... GREAT.

THE SHOCK MUST'VE BEEN TOO MUCH FOR HER.

WHAT NOW, RYOU?

MMM...

HELLO! YOU AWAKE YET?

In front of this cute guy!!

a Mew... that...what happened after that?

UM... I...

The ears...

...and tail are gone.

Wait a minute...

WHEN I SURPRISED YOU IN THE KITCHEN, YOU SLIPPED AND GOT CAKE ALL OVER YOU.

I DON'T REMEMBER...

I'M SORRY FOR FRIGHTENING YOU EARLIER.

I THOUGHT THERE WAS A THIEF OR SOMETHING.

I DIDN'T MEAN TO SCARE YOU LIKE THAT.

Mya?

REALLY? YOU DON'T REMEMBER WHAT HAPPENED?

HUH?

WAS HIDING THE TRUTH FROM HER A GOOD DECISION?

I HOPE SO.

WHAT SHOULD WE DO, RYOU?

FIRST THING TO DO IS DEACTIVATE THE MEW MEW POWER.

ぱぁああああ

BUT...

LET'S JUST SEE HOW IT GOES FOR A WHILE.

HUH?

SHE CHANGED...

BUT I'LL LEAVE THIS WITH HER...JUST IN CASE.

WE'D BETTER NOT TELL HER ANYTHING THAT HAPPENED. SHE'D FLIP OUT.

...BACK TO NORMAL.

TIME WILL TELL...

WILL SHE BE THE NEXT TOKYO MEW MEW...

THAT'S R2003.

YES.

R2000-- MASHA-- WENT TO LONDON WITH ICHIGO.

Masha is going with Ichigo!

Masha is going with Ichigo!

...THE NEWEST LIGHT FOR THE EARTH?

TOP PRIORITY FOR YOU IS TO EXAMINE HOW TWO DIFFERENT GENES GOT INTO ONE HUMAN BODY.

RYOU!!

SHE'LL BE FINE AS LONG AS R2003 IS WITH HER.

OOH...

GOOD MORNING, BERRY!

Kitchen noises...

YOU MUST HAVE SLEPT WELL.

MORNING, DAD.

YEAH... THE NOISE YOU WERE MAKING WOKE ME UP.

YOU HARDLY EVER GET UP ON YOUR OWN.

THANKS!
SEE YA!

Something
strange...

...is going on...

WOOOOW!

YOU'VE GOTTA JOIN THE GYMNASTICS CLUB!

THE BASKETBALL TEAM!

NO! THE TRACK CLUB NEEDS YOU MORE!

THAT WAS AMAZING, BERRY!

SO COOL!

...is happening to me?!

Wh-what in the world..!

51

Came down from the roof

TASUKU!!!

YES, MA'AM! ♡

MISS SHIRA-YUKI.

YOUR FACE IS RED. DO YOU HAVE A FEVER?

YEAH! AND A HEADACHE, TOO.

W-what's Tasuku doing here?!

I'LL BE FINE, BUT I'D BETTER GO STRAIGHT TO THE NURSE!

ARE YOU ALL RIGHT?

HEE HEE. UM...THANKS.

YOU RUN AMAZINGLY FAST, BERRY.

I GOTTA ADMIT, THIS IS A REALLY IMPRESSIVE PRIVATE SCHOOL!

MY SCHOOL KIND OF SUCKS IN COMPARISON.

LISTEN TO ME!

WHAT IN THE WORLD ARE YOU DOING HERE?! WHAT IF SOMEONE SEES YOU?!

I MEAN--

I'VE GOTTA GET BACK TO CLASS RIGHT AWAY!

MY TEACHER THINKS I'VE JUST GONE TO THE NURSE'S OFFICE, AND MY BAG'S STILL IN THE CLASSROOM...

H-HOLD ON A SEC!

EHHHH?!

OKAY, THEN! LET'S GO!

THERE ARE FIVE TOKYO MEW MEW SIGNALS.

WHAT'S WRONG?

STRANGE...

IT'S STRANGE...

THERE MUST BE SOME KIND OF MALFUNCTION.

WHY DON'T YOU USE IT AS A RESEARCH OPPORTUNITY?

NO WAY! THERE SHOULD BE ONLY FOUR SIGNALS RIGHT NOW.

THE STRONGEST ONE, MEW ICHIGO, WENT TO LONDON, RIGHT?

DUKE?

OUR CHIMERA ANIMA PET IN THE BASEMENT...

THIS SHOULD BE A GOOD CHANCE FOR HIM TO GET SOME EXERCISE.

Hee hee!

...HE SEEMS A BIT BORED.

HA HA... AFTER LAUGHING SO MUCH...

...I'M NOT WORRIED ABOUT ANYTHING ANYMORE.

THANK YOU SO MUCH, TASUKU!

I GUESS SO!

THAT'S BECAUSE I KNOW IN MY HEART HOW TO MAKE YOU SMILE!

AHHH!!!

WHAT I WAS DOING WAS ALMOST TOO FAR FOR CHILDHOOD FRIENDSHIP.

OH BOY, THAT WAS CLOSE!

I'LL BE RIGHT BACK!

TASUKU!

Alrighty then! I'll go get something for you!

No, I'm okay for now.

Huh?

I'm mega thirsty.

I'll bet you're thirsty, too.

Waaahh!
He discovered
my secret!!

Now what
am I gonna
do?!

WELL... THIS...

That's right!

...IS A CHARM!!

THAT'S RIGHT!

A CHARM?

Ah!

YEP.

SO YOU SAW IT, DID YOU?

A TAIL, WEAR A *TAIL!* YOU WERE BORN ON JANUARY FIFTH, A CAPRICORN, WITH BLOOD TYPE O. YOUR *LOVE LIFE* WILL IMPROVE IF YOU WEAR THE NEWEST TREND, A *CHARM TAIL!* YOU WILL BE ASKED OUT ON A DATE BY A *BOY* YOU'VE BEEN INTERESTED IN!! AND YOU'LL GET YOUR *TRUE LOVE!!*

...THAT'S WHAT SHE TOLD ME, ANYWAY. UM...YEAH.

TO TELL YOU THE TRUTH, LAST NIGHT, MY GREAT-GRANDMOTHER, *MADEMOISELLE PULI PULI,* UM...YEAH, UM...SHE'S A *MYSTERIOUS FORTUNE-TELLER,* AND SHE APPEARED BY MY BEDSIDE...

ERK.

No go...

THAT'S NOT WHAT I'M TALKING ABOUT!

TO TELL YOU THE TRUTH, I'M THE ONE WHO DROPPED AN ICE CREAM ONTO YOUR SHOES THAT ONE TIME...

NOT THAT!

AH HA HA... GUESS I HAVE TO TELL YOU NOW.

I CAN TELL-- SOMETHING'S UP.

WHY ARE YOU SO WORRIED AND KEEPING IT TO YOURSELF?!

GRAAAH!

Tasuku...

BERRY.

OF COURSE, THE DOWN-SIDE IS THAT ALIENS KEEP ATTACKING ME...

There's no way...

THAT'S WHY...

...I CAN'T BE WITH YOU... ANYMORE...

...we can treat each other the same way we always did ever again...

BERRY, YOU LOOK SUPER CUTE AS A MEW MEW!

3

It was one of my friends who originally gave me the idea for the casting in these illustrations. I got so psyched by the idea that I decided to draw them. Do you like them? Each character fits their role well, don't you think?

Lovestruck village leader's daughter Mint

WELL, I FINALLY HUGGED YOU FOR THE DAY, SO LET'S GO HOME NOW!

WAIT A MINUTE!

THAT'S ALL? JUST *HUH*?

HUH?

AND...

OH NO! ♡

MY HEARING'S SO GOOD NOW, I CAN EVEN HEAR WHEN A TOILET FLUSHES IN YOUR HOUSE.

YOU NEVER KNOW WHEN YOU'LL BE ATTACKED BY AN ALIEN...

HOW CONVE-NIENT!

AND I CAN JUMP HIGHER THAN TEN METERS!

And...

...AS LONG AS YOU'RE WITH ME.

WHAT'S WRONG WITH YOU?

AND I'M CRAVING CARROTS CONSTANTLY!

HOW COULD I QUIT BEING YOUR FRIEND JUST BECAUSE YOU BECAME THE LATEST MEW MEW?

DON'T UNDER-ESTIMATE ME!

Tasuku...

81

83

OF COURSE, IT'S OUT OF SEASON, BUT I WOULD LOVE TO TASTE SOME FRESH, WILD GAME. A WILD ANIMAL!

AND THOUGH THIS L'AMI DU CHAMBERTIN CHEESE HAS A DEEP FLAVOR, IT SEEMS TO BE A BIT TOO RIPE.

BY THE WAY, THIS LANGOUSTINE PAUPIETTE... IT'S DELICIOUS, BUT THE SAUCE IS A TAD TOO STRONG.

NOW... WHO'S GOING TO CATCH IT?

I'M QUITE LOOKING FORWARD TO TASTING IT.

BUT THINGS COULD GET A LITTLE NAUGHTY.

OH! I KNOW THE PERFECT WILD ANIMAL FOR YOU!

DUKE.

ONE THAT'S VERY HEALTHY AND ACTIVE-- AND HOPS!

WHATEVER YOU SAY, YOU'RE STILL YOU, BERRY.

A T-TAS-MANIAN WOLF! I WAS JUST WONDERING IF I COULD HAVE ONE FOR A PET!

EH? AH! ERR...

GOOD MORNING! BERRY?

Tas...?

TASUKU...

Whisper

...just keeps getting...

Oh.

It would be kind of tough to have an extinct animal as a pet.

The Tasmanian wolf is extinct.

Seriously.

Tasuku's rep...

...I'D LIKE TO PLAY AN EASY GAME WITH ALL OF YOU SO WE CAN GET TO KNOW EACH OTHER BETTER.

I PREFER NOT TO BE JUDGED MERELY ON MY REPUTATION.

FIRST OF ALL...

UMM, I REALLY SHOULD GET PERMISSION FROM THE SUPERINTENDENT...

I NEED TO DO THIS GAME WITH JUST A FEW PEOPLE AT A TIME. MAY I USE A DIFFERENT CLASSROOM FOR THIS?

UM, ER... ACTUALLY, I THINK THE LABORATORY IS AVAILABLE.

...IS THAT A "NO?"

THANK YOU SO MUCH FOR YOUR COOPERATION.

WELL THEN, I'D LIKE TO HAVE TEN STUDENTS AT A TIME MOVE TO THE LABORATORY.

EEEEEK!

NOW, TELL ME...

WHAT DOES THIS LOOK LIKE TO YOU?

PHOTO SLIDES?

?

Snap

LET'S BEGIN OUR VERY SPECIAL GAME NOW!

VERY GOOD.

LET ME SEE...A RIBBON? IT KIND OF LOOKS LIKE A BUTTERFLY, TOO.

THIS IS A RORSCHACH PSYCHOLOGICAL TEST.

THERE ARE MULTIPLE ANSWERS, SINCE IT LOOKS A BIT DIFFERENT TO EVERYONE.

EVEN THOUGH YOU'RE ALL LOOKING AT THE SAME THING, A SLIGHTLY DIFFERENT IMPRESSION IS BORN IN EACH PERSON'S MIND.

The Rorschach Test, invented by a Swiss psychiatrist in 1921, evaluates a patient's responses to 10 unique inkblot designs. It helps to determine personality types and detect psychological disorders.

COOL! THE FIRST GROUP OF TEN CAME BACK!

YOU WANNA GO NEXT WITH US, BERRY?

SURE.

Preparation Room

He must've realized I wasn't paying much attention to him earlier...

LET'S SEE...

O-OKAY.

Oops.

YOU'RE GOING TO THE PREPARATION ROOM.

MR. AKIZUKI WANTS YOU TO GET MORE SLIDES.

WHERE CAN I FIND SLIDES?

A man...
when did he
come in?

WHO ARE
YOU?!

Hello! It's me, Ikumi!

Long time no see! How do you do? Nice to meet you--Ikumi here!
Welcome to Volume One of *Tokyo Mew Mew a la Mode.*
Even though this is volume one of the story, it seems like Volume Eight for me,
since I've produced a total of seven volumes of *Tokyo Mew Mew* before this.

Right now, I'm working on a project for the November issue. It's a sunny day and I should probably be doing my laundry, but the deadline for the manga is coming up! ☆

There's only a short time left before the deadline, so things have been hectic, but my staff and I are doing our best! We need some good music CDs when we're stuck in this kind of situation.

I hope you enjoy Volume One of *Tokyo Mew Mew a la Mode!* ♡ ♡

THIS IS...

...DAIKAN-YAMA JUNIOR HIGH... BERRY SHIRAYUKI'S SCHOOL.

That Café Mew Mew...

...where Mr. Shirogane is.

Wait a minute!

I know where I need to go!

What's happening?

What's really going on?

OH!

WELL, UM, I COULDN'T FIND THE SLIDES...

WHAT HAVE YOU BEEN DOING? MR. AKIZUKI ALREADY FINISHED HIS LECTURE.

SAKURAKO? KAORUKO?

Is it just me?

...I BELIEVE WE'VE GOTTEN TO KNOW EACH OTHER WELL ENOUGH BY NOW.

WELL...

Well, I guess I could go to Café Mew Mew after school.

LET'S HEAD BACK TO THE CLASS-ROOM.

These two girls are acting even more weird than usual.

I'M SORRY. I COULDN'T FIND THE SLIDE YOU WERE TALKING ABOUT...

YOU'RE LATE, MY DEAR.

OH, UM, THANK YOU SO MUCH.

IS IT SUCH A BIG DEAL?

SO I'LL HAVE TO GIVE YOU MY SPECIAL LECTURE AFTER SCHOOL.

I SEE. EVERYONE EXCEPT YOU HAS ALREADY HAD MY LECTURE.

BUT YOU'RE STILL MY STUDENT, EVEN THOUGH I'M JUST HERE FOR A SHORT TIME.

HE'S SUCH A GENTLEMAN.

Huh?

WOW, MR. AKIZUKI'S SO KIND!

Y-YEAH.

Oh no...

I'LL SEE YOU AFTER SCHOOL, MISS BERRY SHIRAYUKI.

Why do I have to stay late on a day like this?!

Squeak

Boing!

HERE I COME!

: : : : : : : :

4

Actually, the Mew Mew calendar project existed before I was assigned *Tokyo Mew Mew a la Mode.* At first I had no clue what I was even going to write about in *a la Mode.* On that note, I'd have to say my favorite project has been the calendar. I wanted to make new stories for both projects, though! The story I was going to write for the calendar is totally different from the casting in these illustrations. I hope I can create a new manga from it.

Shrine Maiden Lettuce

ISN'T IT KINDA RUDE TO SUDDENLY ATTACK A STRANGER?

...AREN'T THEY?

THINGS ARE GETTING WEIRDER AND WEIRDER...

THIS CONCLUDES OUR CLASSES FOR THE DAY.

Y-YES!

MS. BERRY? PLEASE GO TO THE LABORATORY NOW.

DEAR MR. AKIZUKI IS WAITING FOR YOU.

Did she just call him dear?

Wait a minute...

ARE YOU READY FOR ME, MISS SHIRAYUKI?

The students going ga-ga was bad enough... but the teachers?

MR. AKIZUKI?

YOU HAVE SUCH BEAUTIFUL HAIR.

A PERFECT BLONDE.

NOW, SIT DOWN AND JUST RELAX.

O-OKAY...

. . . .

MY GRANDPA... UM, MY GRANDFATHER IS FRENCH... AND...

BROWN... BUT IN THIS LIGHT THEY LOOK ALMOST DARK RED.

YOUR EYE COLOR IS AMAZING, TOO...

Ah!

OUCH!!

NO!

OH DEAR.

?!

YOU'RE ONE TOUGH BUNNY, LITTLE WITCH.

I WAS GOING TO BE NICE AND GIVE YOU A GRACEFUL DEATH, HYPNOTIZING YOU WITH SWEET DREAMS...

...BECAUSE, AFTER ALL, I CAN BE A NICE GUY, TOO.

My legs are so wobbly...

INDEED.

!!

I'M GOING TO GIVE MY LITTLE BUNNY A SHOWER OF DEATH.

...ROYAL HIGHNESS?!

IT'S RABBIT SEASON.

I SUPPOSE I SHOULD ENLIST THE HELP OF MY BEAUTIFUL FOLLOWERS...

Huff huff

5

I know I keep talking about the calendar, but I drew some other illustrations I wanted to chat about. I worked three times harder on this one compared to the first two calendars. Because of this, I feel like I definitely made the illustrations better. I love improving my work—it makes me feel great!

Circus Performer Pudding

SIGH!

THE TROUBLE'S ALREADY STARTED!

WHERE THE HECK IS BERRY? URGH!

MR. AKIZUKI IS WAITING FOR YOU...

RIGHT THIS WAY, BERRY.

....

THIS ROOM MUST BE FOR THE DRAMA CLUB.

SORRY, BUT...

TASUKU?!

...SHE'S MINE!

You think so? So do I!

Oddly enough, that uniform looks good on you...

WHAT DO YOU EXPECT TO DO, WITH ALL MY FOLLOWERS SURROUNDING YOU?

RUN AWAY, TASUKU... YOU STILL HAVE A CHANCE TO ESCAPE...

UM, BERRY? I'M NO COWARD OR ANYTHING, BUT I'M OUT-NUMBERED WITH ABOUT A ZERO-PERCENT CHANCE OF WINNING.

So what the heck should I do now?

Hmph!

FOOLS! THE FRIEND OF A BUNNY IS JUST ANOTHER BUNNY.

THE MEW MEW POWER WAS CREATED TO HELP OTHERS.

OKAY, I TRANSFORMED... BUT HOW DO I SAVE MY CLASSMATES?!

NOW LET'S RESCUE THEM!!

YOUR WISH TO HELP YOUR FRIENDS WILL BE EXPRESSED NATURALLY THROUGH YOUR POWER.

B-BUT...

BERRY! BELIEVE IN YOURSELF!!

SHE DID IT!

RIBBON LOVEBERRY CHECK!!

HOW DARE YOU SCAR MY BEAUTIFUL FACE?! STUPID BUNNY!

UGH!

AWW, MR. WHITE FACE IS STARTING TO GET A LITTLE CRANKY!!

WHAT'S THAT?

I WON'T LET ANY OF YOU LEAVE HERE ALIVE!

ROYAL HIGHNESS, YOU ANGER WAY TOO EASILY.

YOU'VE LOST THIS ROUND, ROYAL HIGHNESS. GIVE UP.

ANOTHER ENEMY?

I'D SAY THIS GAME IS OFFICIALLY OVER.

130

YOUR CLASS-MATES SHOULD BE FINE NOW.

MEANWHILE, YOU'D BETTER COME WITH US...

URGH...

KAROUKO! SAKURAKO!

TOP

YOU, TOO...

COME WITH YOU WHERE?

THIS IS...

WHERE ARE WE GOING?

...THE SUPERIN-TENDENT'S OFFICE?

Superintend

Ehhhh?!

AS OF TODAY, YOU ARE THE NEW LEADER OF TOKYO MEW MEW.

And on top of that...

I'M THEIR LEADER NOW?

YES. YOU'RE NOW THE LEADER OF TOKYO MEW MEW.

Wow...

TOTALLY RIGHT, PUDDING.

LADY ZAKURO!

You can be so crabby!

IT'S SO COOL WE'RE ALL GOING TO SCHOOL TOGETHER!

I'M SO HAPPY!

WHATEVER. I DOUBT I'LL BE ABLE TO COME TO SCHOOL MUCH ANYWAY.

I still have my modeling job.

I GET TO GO TO THE SAME SCHOOL AS LADY ZAKURO!

ZZP

TASUKU?!

WOULD YOU MIND EXPLAINING A BIT MORE, SO WE CAN UNDERSTAND?

Tasuku
(Disguised as a girl)

LET'S SAVE THE SERIOUS TALK FOR LATER.

OKAY, OKAY.

TIME TO TOUR YOUR SCHOOL!

The Tokyo Mew Mew family!

....

MR. SHIRO-GANE.

SURE, RYOU.

KEIICHIROU...

...MIND GOING BACK TO THE HOUSE BY YOURSELF?

WHAT IS IT YOU WANT TO SAY?

I DON'T HAVE TIME TO WASTE.

YOU...

I'VE BEEN PREPARED FOR THAT EVER SINCE I STARTED THIS PROJECT.

AH!

TASUKU!!

I WONDER WHY TASUKU HASN'T COME OUT YET?

I WAS WAITING FOR YOU, OF COURSE!

BERRY? WHY ARE YOU HERE?

SO... THANK YOU.

The other members of Tokyo Mew Mew asked me to go to the café with them, but...

I HADN'T THANKED YOU YET.

BERRY...

144

Mysterious Ninja Zakuro

YOU GUYS LOOK SO PRETTY!

THIS IS ACTUALLY A PRETTY NICE SCHOOL.

THANK YOU.

AND WE ALL HAVE THE SAME UNIFORM!

HEY, THAT GIRL LOOKS LIKE THE MODEL ZAKURO FUJIWARA!

THE GIRLS AROUND HER ARE REALLY GOOD-LOOKING, TOO.

THEY'RE A FEAST FOR MY EYES.

Everyone notices these girls.

148

ピクッ

COME TO ME NOW...

...OR I'LL BE FORCED TO KILL EVERYONE.

COME TO ME, MEW BERRY.

I hear someone's voice!

WHAT IS THIS...?

HUH?

BERRY?

Special Thanks!!

T. Matsumoto
M. Omori

A. Okawa
S. Nakazawa
K. Honda
S. Naohara
A. Horie

H. Oikawa

Hara Asumin
M. Sekiya
K. Nakama

M-meeoooww...
(S-some...how...)

WE... DID IT!

SEE YA!!

WELL, THAT'S ENOUGH FOR TODAY, I GUESS. AT LEAST YOU MADE ME LAUGH!

WHAT IN THE WORLD HAPPENED TO YOU?

OH, GIRLS...

BERRY!!

Meoooww. (I'm sorry...)

DIDN'T I WARN YOU NOT TO JOIN THE FIGHT...

...RIGHT AFTER BEING ON VACATION?!

ICHIGO! HAVE YOU FORGOTTEN THAT ONE OF YOUR WORST EXPERIENCES HAPPENED WHEN YOU BECAME A CAT INSTEAD OF A MEW MEW?!

Ichigooo!

That's how the aliens caught you!

I love string!

Meoooww!

And how you ended up chasing that mouse-shaped alien.

Mint got stuck in the mud because of Ichigo.

HOW COME YOU'RE SO? BACK IN JAPAN, ICHIGO?

AHH! FINALLY BACK IN MY NORMAL BODY!

HUH?

Ichigo can't become human again until she kisses someone. What a pain!

Victim cat caught by Ichigo

DIDN'T I TELL YOU THAT?

OH! MY STUDY ABROAD WAS ONLY FOR FOUR MONTHS, SILLY.

ANYWAY...

おろおろ

I DIDN'T KNOW!

WHAT WAS THAT?!

164

WELCOME
BACK,
ICHIGO!!

Pointless Bloomers Drawing

When I was working on the story for the November 2003 issue, I drew this illustration for no reason. At first, I wanted to draw a girl with an American waitress dress and rollerblades, but then one of my staff said, "I want to see a girl wearing bloomers." So this illustration came about because of that. And it has nothing to do with what I'm talking about, but I love drawing illustrations of two girls hugging each other. Again, for no apparent reason—I don't know why!

WELCOME!

OH! WE ALREADY HAVE TWO CUSTOMERS!

WHAT?!

FIRST, LET ME GIVE YOU A TOUR OF THE CAFÉ.

WHY AM I ALWAYS THE ONLY ONE WHO DOES ANY WORK?!

EEEEEEEK!

BERRY! YOU READY?

Huff
huff

WH-WHERE'S BERRY?

HEY, YOU!

WE ALWAYS HAVE AFTER-NOON TEA AT THIS HOUR.

THEY'RE DEFINITELY STRONGER THAN I REALIZED.

THOSE MEW MEWS ARE PRETTY TOUGH.

What's wrong with me?

Why is Tasuku making my heart beat so hard?

IS THAT SO?

WE NEED TO DO SOMETHING, OR WE WON'T BE ABLE TO MAKE THE DUKE'S WISH COME TRUE.

W-WHAT WAS THAT?

IF THE POWER OF OUR ENEMY IS SO ENORMOUS, PERHAPS WE JUST NEED TO USE IT WISELY.

DUKE?

DUKE...

IN THIS WORLD, THERE ARE FAR MORE ENEMIES WITHOUT THE POWERS OF THE MEW MEWS.

...you're...

THEY ARE WEAK, BUT THEIR NUMBERS ARE UNLIMITED.

But because of that, we were discriminated against and hated by our parents and friends.

We were all born with powers normal people don't have...

...super-natural powers.

Finally...

...we were all sent to one boarding school.

The truth is, we were almost abandoned.

I MADE SURE THE DOOR WAS LOCKED SO NO ONE ELSE COULD COME IN.

WHO ARE YOU?!

...I HEARD A VOICE CALLING FOR HELP.

FROM THIS ROOM...

YOU ARE ALL SO LONELY.

BUT YOU DON'T WANT TO BLAME YOUR PARENTS OR FRIENDS.

NO ONE WILL EVER ACCEPT YOUR EXISTENCE.

NO ONE WILL EVER ACCEPT YOU AS HUMANS.

We met the Duke.

...we decided to give you our all.

That day...

...when we met you...

I JUST CAME UP WITH AN INTERESTING IDEA, DUKE.

WE FINALLY FINISHED OUR WORK FOR TODAY!

IT WAS SUCH AN EASY DAY OF WORK, EVEN IF IT WAS A BIT CROWDED THANKS TO BERRY'S BOYFRIEND.

THANKS!

I AGREE! THANK GOODNESS FOR THAT BOY PITCHING IN!

HE'S SO COOL WITH THOSE ROLLERBLADES!

Ah! He put his arm around her shoulder! They're in love!!

Aww, don't be shy, Berry.

But he's not my boyfriend...

You idiot!

Masaya...

ICE CREAM, PLEASE!

HERE YOU ARE, MISS.

...I wonder what you're doing right now.

BUT I LOVE HIS ICE CREAM! CHEAP AND GOOD!

HEE HEE. I DIDN'T ACTUALLY UNDERSTAND WHAT THAT MAN SAID TO ME.

YOUR PRONUN-CIATION'S IMPROVING.

...BUT I CAN FEEL THIS.

I DON'T HAVE THE POWER I HAD WHEN I WAS DEEP BLUE...

I SOMETIMES MISS THE DESSERTS FROM CAFE MEW MEW...

...A DANGER IS COMING.

TO THE EARTH...TO THE MEW MEWS...

YOU'VE BEEN FEELING THE SAME THING... HAVEN'T YOU, ICHIGO?

HOLD IT RIGHT THERE!!

Smile

I, SWEET JULIET, WILL TAKE IT FROM HERE.

SORRY, MR. AN-NOUNCER.

H-HEY! LOOK!

CAN IT BE?!

EVERYONE! IT'S THE MEW MEWS! TOKYO MEW MEW IS HERE!

WH-WHAT?! THE MEW MEWS ARE HERE?!

pfft

MEW MEW!

Here we go!

MEW MEW!

MEW MEW!

MEW MEW!

NOW! LET'S CHEER THEM ON WITH OUR LOUDEST VOICES!

EVERYONE! LET'S PUT ALL OUR HOPES WITH THE MEW MEWS!

WHAT'S GOING ON?

MEW MEW!

MEW MEW!

MEW MEW!

OH, BY THE WAY, I'M HERE TAKING OVER FOR THE ANNOUNCER WHO JUST FAINTED. I'M YOUR LOVELY REPORTER, OTOME SAKURAGASUMI!!

EVERYONE'S TALKING ABOUT THE MEW MEWS.

I-I KNOW!

Every channel's showing the Tokyo Mew Mew battle!!

Wow!

Beep

Beep

The TV remote

BERRY! TODAY... YOU AND ME... LET'S...

MORNING, BERRY!

I'm so embarrassed... even if they don't know it was me!!

GOSH! THEY'RE SHOWING MY PICTURE AGAIN!

Killing time.

I'll just write whatever I'm feeling right now.

Number one: The Calendar

I was happy to have another book signing with my fans this year. But I was even happier about the sale of this year's 2004 Tokyo Mew Mew Calendar.☆ It will be sold for three consecutive years. I'm super-excited and drew many, many illustrations for it, since I had no time to work that much last year. ☆ I even retouched and redrew some illustrations from the past. I was sitting in front of my computer most of this time. I thought my method of drawing 13 illustrations at the same time would finish the job faster. But I haven't even finished one illustration since I started the calendar project more than a month ago (sweat, sweat). While I was working on this project, I started getting used to my new computer. I started thinking, "Hey! This illustration can be retouched and totally improved with this new technique!" or, "Oh! I really want to draw something new like this!!" But the deadline for both the calendar and this manga is only a few days away...so I'd better kick into gear soon (sweat).

Number two: Mew Mew Merchandise ☆

I recently realized that I have so much *Tokyo Mew Mew* merchandise at my house. It's probably the most I'll ever have for a character I created. (And I don't even take very good care of it!! I use up so many Mew Mew dishes so I won't have to wash them, hee hee.) And I still have so many products stuck in cardboard boxes. I dream about organizing all of them one day (laugh).

Number three: My House ☆

I feel like I've found a place where I can finally live in peace. Of course, I can't live here forever, since this place is just another rental apartment. But this is the first place I have chosen on my own. Until now, I would choose a place because someone said, "Why don't you live around there?" or, "Why don't you move near my place?" And I'd always say, "Well, I guess I can." Originally I moved to Tokyo from Osaka for work, so I just thought, "The most important thing is that I can work at my place." But one day, my boss asked me, "Why don't you just live in your favorite city?" So I decided to seriously look for a new place. At first, I looked for a city I could love. And, eventually, I found this place! It's far from the train station, but the environment is great! It's a secret where I live now, though! I just want to stay here as long as I can and live happily ever after...that's my wish!

Number Four: Stuffed Animals ☆

Some of the things I covet most are stuffed animals. Although I didn't use to be interested in them, I started getting into them this year. Every time I go out, I always check out the UFO Catcher (the claw) at the arcade. I know it's probably cheaper to buy it at a toy store instead of trying to catch it from the crane (since I never seem to win), but I can't stop thinking about those animals behind the glass! There was this puppet of a Panda in a commercial for some tea company that I wanted so badly and could never seem to get. (Yes, that panda that kisses! ☆) By the way, I've never caught anything from that darn claw in my life. Boo hoo.

Postscript ☆

Since *Tokyo Mew Mew* became a TV Anime, I have had the most hectic life, with so much work last year. I still enjoy the work, even though I'm so busy now. But even though the most hectic time has finally passed, I still don't feel like I have much free time. I guess I should appreciate that I finally have time to cook, do some laundry, and have tea with my friends. ☆

Last year, it was so much work to even cook dinner while I was on a project. But I guess the reason I always felt I had no time was that I put too many different projects into my schedule. Someone actually said, "Ikumi, you are driving yourself off a cliff!" That person was right. Because even now, I still think I should be able to make some free time by working at such and such a pace—so, like a fool, I add something else to my schedule. Do you think I'm abusing myself?

I think it's great to have so many things that I want and try to do. I feel alive when I have something I can try to do my best. Even though my life is so hectic, I still have so much power to go on! Everyone, make the most of your lives along with me!

In conclusion...
Special thanks to the people who joined me in the process of creating this manga, the people who helped me to produce it and the people who are reading it...thank you sooooo much!!

Always be positive!
5:20 P.M. 9.12.2003 Mia Ikumi

DON'T MISS THE NEXT VOLUME OF

TOKYO MEW MEW
A LA MODE

The girls from Mew Mew are back with a vengeance. But this time they're up against their worst enemy ever--their fans!!! Someone is slipping subliminal messages about the Mews into television shows, the Internet and more. With not-so-friendly statements like "Down with the Mew Mew," and "Hate the Mews!" slipping into the media, everyone who watches TV is about to go into a trance where they hate anything and everything Mew! Even Mew Berry's crush buys into the Mew Mew-hating frenzy. What in the world is a Mew to do?

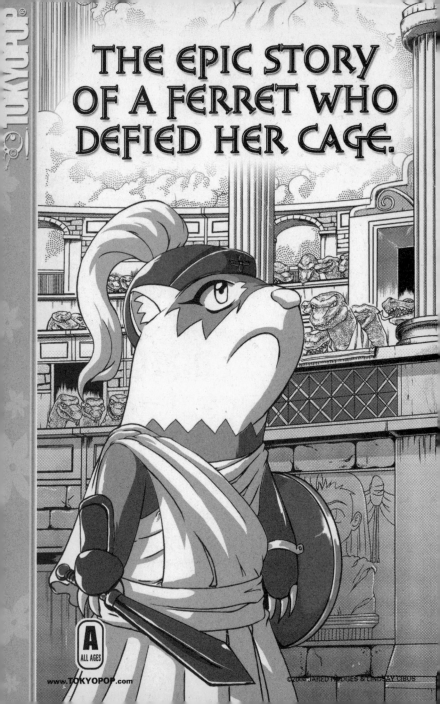

THE EPIC STORY OF A FERRET WHO DEFIED HER CAGE.

STOP!

This is the back of the book.
You wouldn't want to spoil a great ending!

This book is printed "manga-style," in the authentic Japanese right-to-left format. Since none of the artwork has been flipped or altered, readers get to experience the story just as the creator intended. You've been asking for it, so TOKYOPOP® delivered: authentic, hot-off-the-press, and far more fun!

DIRECTIONS

If this is your first time reading manga-style, here's a quick guide to help you understand how it works.

It's easy... just start in the top right panel and follow the numbers. Have fun, and look for more 100% authentic manga from TOKYOPOP®!